Winning the Wardrobe War

Discovering a Look You Love Without Breaking the Bank

A Style Guide for Busy Women

Rainah Davis
Tori Jones
Somanetha Moulate
Ashley Brooks

First edition. December 2024.

Cover design concept:
Rainah Davis
Cover design artwork:
Brittany Oliver

Editing:
Start Write Team—Gerald C. Simmons, Tiara Brown, Alora White

Print ISBN: 978-1-970179-07-1
eBook ISBN: 978-1-970179-26-2

**Printed by GCS Publishing.
Atlanta, GA, USA.**

Neither the publisher, author, or contributors are engaged in giving professional advice or services to the individual reader. While the author and contributors have made every effort to provide accurate internet addresses at the time of publication, neither the publisher nor the author assumes any responsibility for errors or changes that occur after publication.

For Author Speaking, Booking, or Bulk Copies:

Rainah Davis
hello@raindrop-creative.com
StartWrite Office:
admin@startwriteaway.com

Dedication

*To our daughters, granddaughters, and
every woman determined to show up
as her absolute best, this book is for you.
May you always be determined to dress for
where you are headed and never based on
where you have been.*

Table of Contents

Introduction

"When you look good, you feel good, when you feel good, you play good, and when you play good, they pay good."
– Coach Deion Sanders

I used a version of this quote for years before knowing where it originated. Imagine my delight when I heard Coach Deion Saunders say it during one of his many interviews as coach of the Colorado Buffaloes. Now, you may not be as flamboyant or flashy as "Prime Time," but I encourage you to find a style that fits your personality, budget, and future. In particular, it is easy for women to get lost in caring for everyone other than themselves. Unfortunately for them, the last thing that suffers is their appearance. I know this too well.

My name is Rainah Davis, and I am so excited to be on this journey with you! I am a wife, mother, bonus mom, daughter, and grandmother. I am serious about living a fulfilling and prosperous life. Equally important to me is helping as many women as possible reach their ideal lives. Over the years, I've recognized that one of the most troubling aspects of daily life for women involves appearance and wardrobe. Lacking confidence in our appearances holds us back in so many ways. We avoid seeking career advancement, shun business opportunities, and refuse to do many things social media-related due to "how we look."

While some of these responses are natural, often, these feelings of inadequacy and insecurity spring from wells of trauma. Whether you used to like how you looked in college but now you don't; or if you love your appearance but lack the resources to finance a quality wardrobe; or if you are actively working on weight loss (or gain) but don't know how to dress for your current size and shape—this book was created for you. I have teamed up with some incredible ladies to bring you a short book to help you win the wardrobe war and slay your look, all without breaking the bank! It is short, not because we don't have much to share on the subject, but because I know most of you don't have time to read a 200-page book.

Before we get into the good stuff, I think it is fitting that you hear more about my story and why this topic is so crucial to me. Over a decade ago, I went through a highly traumatic divorce. Our children were severely affected by the split. As a result of worrying about our financial well-being, my weight spiraled downward. To clarify, as the mother of four biological children, my weight has always fluctuated. With my first child, I weighed about 106 pounds and considered myself petite. After my last child, my weight increased to 141 pounds—a dramatic increase.

While some people eat more amid a crisis, the opposite occurs for me. When I experience extreme stress, I have a problematic time consuming anything. For example, after my divorce, I lost so much weight that my measurements were size 00. Now, this may sound like a significant problem to have, but it was a pretty unhealthy size for me. I began to struggle to find clothing that fit my petite frame and was often forced to pay for alterations.

Shopping became a hassle and created an additional expense to my wardrobe. Ultimately, being petite presented a series of unfortunate issues for me.

During that time, as an executive assistant to a senior pastor in ministry, I had a highly visible role. Early in my career, I realized that to represent myself and the ministry well, I had to have a wardrobe appropriate for any situation. During this time, I decided to start dressing for *where I was going* rather than *where I had been.* I began to believe that how I carried myself and my outward appearance would contribute to my future success. I decided to invest in fashions that reflect this mindset. I will share more about what I did next and what I suggest you do in chapter one. But first, I want to tell you a little more about the book and introduce you to the incredible ladies who contributed—then, we will dive in!

About This Book

Now that you know a little about me, I want to tell you more about this book and how to use it. First, I mentioned that I have teamed up with a group of dynamic ladies to bring this project to life. The team that authored this book is a collaborative effort between an incredible stylist, a master makeup artist, a certified hair care professional, and yours truly.

The idea of this book was born out of a webinar I did years ago with Kristina Butler of *KB Career Solutions*. She encouraged me to develop the title, and "Winning the Wardrobe War" was born. It was a webinar for busy working women (especially moms) on overcoming the battle of trying to figure out what to wear daily.

In 2024, we have a new challenge: many women work from home. This can make outfit selections more challenging because some people have clothes that no longer fit them or their lifestyles.

Even more tragic are the women sitting on their gifts and talents because they dislike their appearance. Someone needs to see that YouTube channel you refuse to start because you don't like your hair. Someone needs your Instagram insights, Facebook features, or TikTok truth. Yet, we can't get it if you are stuck in a war with your wardrobe and appearance.

Winning the Wardrobe War helps you overcome these challenges by giving you eight easy-to-read chapters. Tori Jones wrote the first six to help you slay your look by addressing your closet, wardrobe, and fashion fundamentals. Along the way, we address cheat codes like dressing for your body type, specialty garments, accessories, and much more! The bonus chapters were written with collaborators Somanetha Moulate and Ashley Brooks. You will love them as much as I do, and I will introduce them to you next. They are going to help you increase your confidence and slay every day!

Meet the Contributors

Tori Jones

Tori J. Jones is a coastal Virginia fashionista who loves God, people, and fashion! Her style philosophy is "to bring out the best in you." She has multiple degrees in fashion marketing and is a college instructor at The Art Institute of Virginia Beach. She also works as an independent fashion stylist and TV wardrobe stylist.

Fashion is not a new passion for Tori. She has loved all things fashion and style for as long as she can remember! Her mother tells stories of how she loved to dress Tori when she was little. Tori was her mom's little live fashion baby doll, and she would change her outfits two or three times per day! Her mother dressed her in everything girly with accessories to match. She recalls having every matching shoe, bow, hat, and handbag at three years old.

As she grew older and began watching TV shows and movies, she always noticed the actors' fashion. It stuck out to Tori more than anything else. Although she went through a "Punky Brewster" phase (where she would wear different color Keds (sneakers) and opposite color socks), for the most part, she was always interested in all things fashionable.

Later in life, Tori was introduced to fashion magazines. She loved what she saw and asked her mom to make things for her if she couldn't find them in stores. Tori would even design clothing and have her mom make them. She started taking fashion marketing classes in high school and worked her first fashion retail job. Tori thrived in this job because she loved putting looks together for people. She also enjoyed how the customers felt once she dressed them.

Upon graduation, Tori pursued studies in fashion retail management, freelance styling, and personal shopping. Though she eventually took some time off to pursue other interests and raise her family, Tori returned to college and earned her fashion marketing and management degrees.

Today, Tori has over twenty years of experience in various fashion-related vocations and even owned a boutique that serviced many clients within a seven-city area. She is also a fashion stylist for many hair designers and beauticians across the eastern U.S. Additionally, much of Tori's work has been published in hair magazines.

Tori has styled musical artists for a few record labels native to the Hampton Roads/Coastal Virginia area. Tori is most excited about her newest specialty, "the wardrobe remix," where she restyles clothing items that clients already own and helps them save money and the planet.

Tori was excited to contribute to this project because fashion is a gift, and she uses it daily for God's glory. She feels that fashion is important because it is a creative outlet that allows her to serve others. As you read the following pages, Tori wants to remind you that "every day is a runway!" So, it is time to walk yours with confidence and style.

Book & Get More Fashion Tips with Tori:
http://torijjones.com
Follow Tori on IG: @the.torijjones

Somanetha Moulate (Sommie)

Somanetha Moulate is a Haitian-American entrepreneur in Atlanta, GA, and the owner of HX Professional. Committed to personal empowerment, health, and wellness, Somanetha strongly believes that makeup is one of the most impactful ways to express yourself and bring out inner confidence in people.

As a young girl challenged with the ideas of what popular culture defined as beauty, Somanetha began a journey to find herself and her own sense of beauty. Somanetha soon learned that makeup is not needed to create beauty. Instead, it is a tool that can help others see themselves and their uniqueness from the inside out.

With a psychology background and bachelor's degree in counseling, Somanetha's passion for *touching* people from the inside out sparked the desire to change how women felt through makeup. As a result, for over eight years, Somanetha has been active in her local community and internationally in ministry, missions, and family counseling.

Additionally, Somanetha has been actively involved in several charitable efforts. She views volunteerism as she always has: a way to inspire others. Her love for artistic creativity and desire to connect with people led to the launch of several brands in the beauty industry.

Book with Sommie: **http://hxprofessional.com**
Follow Sommie on IG: @simplysommie

Ashley Brooks

Ashley Brooks knows the toll of juggling various responsibilities and duties while maintaining the delicate balance of finding time for personal grooming. In response to this dilemma, she blends her expertise as a professional hair stylist, working mother of four, and wife to help others develop regimes, routines, and styles. Her goal is to enable them to enjoy the best of both worlds.

Ashley has leveraged the invaluable insights she has cultivated over the years. Ever since discovering her passion for hair styling at six, she has empowered her clients to sustain their healthy hair journeys intentionally. As a Certified Hair Loss Technician, Ashley specializes in natural hair blowouts and sew-ins. She translates her well-rounded knowledge of working on all hair types into easy-to-understand anecdotes that are a welcome addition to any self-care routine.

As a native of Durham, North Carolina, Ashley is a graduate of the Durham Beauty Academy. She prides herself on being a point of contact when it comes to hair styling and maintenance haircare matters. You can inquire about her services at Ashley Squared Salon in Durham, NC.

Book with Ashley: **http://ashleysquared.com**
Follow Ashley on IG: @_ashleysquared

CHAPTER 1:

Attack Your Closet

*Do you ever feel like you have nothing
to wear, but you have a whole closet
full of clothes? If so, it is time to attack
your closet!*

I n my introduction, I shared with you how I endured a tough divorce while raising my four daughters as a single mom. I had also started a new job in a high-profile role. During that time, several advisors told me I needed to "revamp" my look for the accepted position. I was making $42,000 a year: I couldn't afford a lot, but I was also over the limit for any assistance.

The very thought of going shopping was stressful, even though I loved all things fashion! Buying clothes for myself was the last of my concerns, considering I had an elementary student, two middle schoolers, and a high schooler to care for daily. Yet, as a woman of faith, I refused to become overwhelmed by everything coming at me all at once. I decided I had to start somewhere, and that place was my closet.

Nothing will change your life like not having to sift through racks of clothes that no longer fit your body, your life, or the person you are trying to become. So, before we get into how you can win your wardrobe war, I need you to get some big trash bags (preferably the big black ones meant for leaves) because this is about to get *real*. You are about to attack your closet in four ways:

1. Purge it
2. Purpose it
3. Pair It
4. Pass it on

Getting through this process is a must before we buy a single thing! Attacking your closet is the first thing I want you all to do because it diversifies your clothing options in four distinct ways. This overhaul can be accomplished by **purging, giving purpose, pairing, and passing** clothes on to others. I will explain what each of these concepts means throughout this chapter.

Purge It

If you desire to have a closet that is reflective of your future endeavors, the first thing you have to do is purge what you don't want. An item should be considered purge-worthy if it is something you have never worn and have no plans to wear. This category does not include articles of clothing that have sentimental value to you. A family heirloom item or a favorite shirt (that is now too small but motivates you to wear it again one day) should not be purged. These items still have value and are often irreplaceable, and they can be passed on to other family members. Instead, I am specifically referring to clothes that take up space and have no purpose in your lifestyle. Purging items like these will free up your closet and allow you to create outfits quickly. Also, holding on to clothes that are several sizes too small or too big can harm your self-esteem. You want clothes that are an excellent fit for your current physique. Now, if you have a few items you are using as inspiration to become a specific size and are actively working towards that goal, that is not what I am talking about. I have seen that work as a solid motivator for those on intentional weight loss journeys; just be sure you are not keeping clothes that make you feel bad about the body you have right now. You should be loving the body you have, even if you are working towards a body you want!

Purpose It

After purging, the next step is to *give your remaining clothes a purpose*. This activity can be done by identifying which outfits can be worn professionally, for date night, as loungewear, or anywhere between. This activity requires categorizing the items into your personal brand style.

For example, there are three aspects to my everyday personal brand. My style is sporty chic, athleisure, and business casual. These are the main aspects of my year-round style. However, I switch sporty to a colorful and playful summer sundress vibe in the summer. Developing your personal brand will make it much easier for you to properly purpose your wardrobe. After you have divided the clothes into categories, go ahead and pair your clothing and accessories.

Pair It

The next step to a highly organized closet is to look at your clothes, shoes, and jewelry and pair the outfits together. Depending on your lifestyle, you can match the items and hang them up in the closet as outfit sets that are ready to wear! Visibly knowing your matches helps set your closet up in a useful order.

For example, I have all long dresses, skirts, and lightweight outerwear together. I have suit jackets and dress pants hanging together. Next, I have blouses in order of sleeveless, short sleeves, and long sleeves together. I also have the colors together for further grouping. This organization allows me to access the items I need quickly. All my jeans, sweats, and athleisure are folded in rows at the top of my closet. That level of organization is optional for everyone, so it is essential that you do what works best for you.

Pass It

Now that you have purged, purposed, and paired all the keepers, it is time to deal with the remaining clothes items. These should be passed on to other individuals who can wear them. Whether you donate them to *Goodwill or Salvation Army* or give them to a family member or friend, passing along unused clothing can help you declutter your space and make room for clothes you want or need. After completing these steps, we can organize and prepare the rest of your closet. You should also consider local shelters and charities that may need gently used items. The clothes that are causing you clutter and frustration could be a tremendous blessing for those in need.

Consider your closet as a toolbox and the clothing inside it as the tools: an organized closet and a proper clothing inventory are effective ways to **win the wardrobe war**. If you look around when you are finished and feel you don't have a full chest of tools, don't worry. This book is designed as a blueprint. The following pages will help you map out your plan to get what you need to look and feel your absolute best!

CHAPTER 2:

Budgets and Brands

Not all of us can afford Gucci, Channel, Prada, and other big designer brands. However, that doesn't mean we can't enjoy luxury items because we absolutely can—AND STAY ON A BUDGET! As a woman who wants to present herself well, you should pay special attention to your overall appearance. Investing in luxury fashion items will help you achieve this because they are made from quality materials, are stylish, and make you look classy.

In this chapter, Tori and I will weigh in on how you can look good at any budget level and which brands are worth splurging on. Check out our Chief Fashionista's fresh take below:

Tori Talks Fashion

The luxury market is big business. It's a way to help with the sustainability crisis looming within ourselves, the fashion industry, and the world. Luxury items typically last longer and are made better, which, in return, becomes an investment. Luxury items may cost more, but the investment you put in is cost per wear. Here is an example of cost per wear: I have a Louis Vuitton bag I paid $165 for twenty years ago. Suppose you divide that by the $165 I spent on it. In that case, it's more than paid for itself versus buying a $10 or $15 bag that (due to low quality and general wear and tear) would've had to be repurchased repeatedly. For this reason, we must compare quality versus quantity.

I cannot stress this enough: beware of cheap clothes with hidden costs. Consider choosing quality fabrics that cost more upfront and buy fewer items overall. A $20 top from a fast fashion outlet will only last you a little while before it gets worn out. You get what you pay for when it comes to cheap clothing.

A top that is ethically made with quality fabrics will last you much longer than the $20 top from the fast fashion shop. These can be harder to find and cost more upfront, but they will last longer. There are many benefits of longer-lasting clothing:

- You spend less time shopping to replace your wardrobe when they wear out.
- You get more value per wear over the lifetime of the item.
- You send fewer textiles to the landfill.

Ultimately, consider the "value" of an item in terms of the cost per wear (cost divided by how many times it will be worn) when purchasing new clothes. Yes, it may cost a few extra dollars upfront, and you need to research a particular brand's quality if you are investing in an item. However, in the meantime, it is best to avoid the bottom-dollar cheapest clothing (especially from online retailers that crank out products at a speedy rate).

Cheaply made clothing tends to look cheap. If you are budget-conscious, try looking at consignment shops for clothes. Here, you can often find quality pieces for medium prices. A bit of luck is involved when you go to consignment shops, but if there is one near you, it's worth a bit of extra time to see what you can find.

We mention many of my favorite stores to shop at below, but here are a few more stores that I would add:

Aritzia, BCBG, and Mango. They all sell jeans, which could be a great alternative to Levi's. Also, H&M has a premium line that provides luxury items at a much better cost. My favorite stores are Zara, Express, Mango, Nasty Gal, and Boohoo for authentic leather items. Even stores like Banana Republic and J. Crew have higher price points than "fast fashion" retailers. Still, they typically have better quality products like wool, cotton, satin, and silk that don't break down as quickly as polyester and synthetic fibers. Regardless, it is possible to look sensational with any given budget. It's less about the cost and more about how you mix and match your closet with creativity and intentionality.

Besos, Tori

Statistics show that consumers in the United States spent more on luxury fashion (up to $25 billion in 2022) than other luxury goods. These numbers prove more people are embracing luxury fashion because of the benefits mentioned (and you can also be one of them).

If you're worried about being unable to afford quality clothing, don't be! You can look good no matter your income bracket. The trick is knowing which items and brands are worth splurging on. I learned this when I lost significant weight after my divorce and was forced to constantly pay more for alterations since I couldn't find clothing that fit my petite frame. Today, I want to share that knowledge with you. Let's dive into affordable and luxury fashion brands for women you should know about.

Zara

We started with Zara because it's a great place to find quality fashionable items, whether you're into trendy or classic pieces. Examples of the items Zara offers include dresses, jumpsuits, belts, bags, trousers, sandals, shoes, sweaters, coats, jeans, vests, skirts, etc. One of the reasons people flock to Zara is because they alternate the items on their display every three to four weeks. This process makes consumers excited to see what items they have next. Usually, new clothing is guaranteed to be available whenever shoppers show up.

Research shows that Zara is the top-searched luxury brand worldwide—a testament to its popularity. Also, it's easy to shop at Zara because they have so many stores (ninety-nine in America alone) and offer online access. We highly recommend using Zara to build your wardrobe with clothing that will make you look professional and classy and represent the woman you strive to be.

Trina Turk

If you're into contemporary fashion, look at Trina Turk. This affordable and luxury brand has its headquarters in Los Angeles, California. So, it incorporates a lot of the coastal feel to its clothing. You can get dresses, swimwear, sleepwear, tops, and accessories from Trina Turk.

Trina (who co-founded the company with her late husband) incorporates bold signature prints, bright colors, glamor, and fabulous fabrications into her clothing. Her clothes are a mixture of modern and vintage looks. If you are looking for ready-to-wear clothes that are stylish and timeless, Trina Turk is the right place for you. What's more? You can get outfits for both formal and casual occasions, shop online, or access their products from their physical stores.

Lacoste

René Lacoste, the famous tennis player, founded Lacoste with businessman André Gillier. The company specializes in men's, women's, and children's clothing. Sometimes, you may need to run a quick errand, walk, or keep warm during the cold seasons and still *look good*. In that case, this is where Lacoste clothing items come into play. Their clothes are sporty but still classy. They sell sweatshirts, polo shirts (which they're most famous for), jackets, T-shirts, sweaters, jumpers, track pants, shoes, bags, and watches. Lacoste is popular because it provides quality apparel at affordable prices.

Levi's

Levi's is on our list of affordable and luxury brands for women because they sell luxurious jeans at affordable prices. I can't tell you the number of times I've bought jeans that are too big, too small, of terrible quality, or do not flatter my body. It was even more complicated when my weight kept fluctuating. And I'm sure I'm not alone.

Getting a great pair of jeans takes work, but it is possible when you shop at Levi's. Who better to trust than the people who invented blue jeans in 1873? And that's precisely what the founder, Levi Strauss, did. Levi's provides classic jeans made from high-quality denim that are durable and pocket-friendly. Additionally, they are environment-friendly. At the time of this publication, they are even more popular due to a collaboration with Queen Bee herself—Beyonce.

Tory Burch

Named after its founder, Tory Burch, this company's clothing represents American luxury. Tory loves color, and she's not afraid to play with them in her designs. You can't miss her collections at New York Fashion Week each year, which are a testament to the quality of her products. She infuses distinctive details into her pieces and draws inspiration from her travels.

Although the brand is known for its handbags, which are manufactured using the finest materials, it also sells tops, accessories, dresses, bottoms, and handbags. Tory wants to empower women by helping them pursue capital and digital resources. That's one of the reasons she started the company in 2004. If you're looking to shop for ageless and versatile clothes from a brand that cares about women, Tory Burch is a great choice.

Michael Kors

You may be surprised to see Michael Kors on this list of affordable and luxury brands, but let me explain. This brand has two segments for different people. The first one, the Michael Kors Collection, consists of expensive luxury items, from handbags to shoes and clothes. This brand is what most people are familiar with.

However, another segment is Michael: Michael Kors Collection. This line provides the same clothing items but at much more affordable prices. The second collection aimed to expand the company's customer base and make more people feel that they're part of Michael Kors' family. I recommend you explore this collection to build your wardrobe because the items are still elegant and of excellent quality.

Michael Kors' clothing items communicate luxury in a way that elevates a woman's look. Michael says that his designs are suited for people with fast-paced lives who still need to look their best. So, if you are a busy woman who needs to dress for success,

Michael Kors can be your go-to luxury ready-to-wear women's brand. The company produces clothes, wallets, shoes, watches, handbags, and jewelry. These pieces are chic and long-lasting, ooze glamour, have attention to detail, and include timeless designs.

Kate Spade New York

Kate Spade New York represents optimistic femininity, according to its two founders, Kate and Andy Spade. Although this brand is popularly known for its handbags, it also sells jewelry, clothes, and home decor items. The company prides itself on including thoughtful details in its pieces to make its items look chic and polished. If your style is modern and sophisticated, you'll love Kate Spade New York clothing items. Additionally, their prices are affordable compared to others for the quality you are receiving. You can buy fall sweaters, jumpsuits, wedding attire, cocktail dresses, and sleepwear from the company. They can dress you for different occasions.

Discounted Retail Fashion Stores

When I started working as an executive assistant for a large church, I knew I needed professional clothes. A friend advised me to check out discount stores like Marshalls and TJ Maxx. She said they offered quality clothing at way lower prices than department stores–and she wasn't wrong. I began to shop around at discount stores like the ones she told me about, as well as Ross; these were retail vendors with quality clothing for a fraction of the price of department stores. Here, I found affordable, professional clothing that I enjoyed wearing. The experience was uplifting and was something I was not accustomed to from living in my small hometown of Goldsboro, North Carolina (even though Goldsboro is on the rise now and has these stores and many more)!

When I first started shopping there almost ten years ago, I was surprised that these stores offered something I had not seen since growing up. These discount retailers offered 'layaway'—a business system that helps customers build their wardrobe and stay within budget by paying for items over time. The setup was perfect for me as I started acquiring new clothes. I invested in this service because it allowed me to have an opportunity to build my wardrobe on a strict budget.

In addition to discount stores and taking advantage of store layaway options, I committed myself to purchasing one dress a month for a year. The process allowed me to look my best on Sundays (our busiest day of the week) and be financially responsible. I would review my finances monthly, set a budget, and purchase items when they went on sale. I rarely ever bought anything that was full price. Aggressive bargain hunting such as this was imperative to help me build an incredible wardrobe that was equally as affordable. If you follow these tips, you can achieve the same outcome.

Time to Look Luxurious on a Budget

In conclusion, you don't need to drain your bank account to afford elegant fashion pieces because reasonable luxury brands exist for women. Any woman can look great on a budget. The most important thing is to know where to shop.

The brands mentioned here will give you chic, timeless, versatile, and durable clothing that will make you look and feel like a million bucks. You can dress your best whether relaxing at home, running an errand, or chairing a meeting. These luxurious brands have various items, from clothes to accessories, providing formal and casual wear.

Here is a list of my favorite stores that typically never fail me in cost or quality:

1. **Nordstrom Rack**
2. **Marshalls/TJMaxx**
3. **H & M**
4. **Express**

My honorable mentions include:

1. **Ross**
2. **Macy's** (my go-to for affordable formal wear & accessories)
3. **DSW**
4. **Belk's**
5. **Old Navy/Gap/Banana Republic**
6. **Target**
7. **JC Penney's**
8. **Burlington Coat Factory**

Special note: a few of my girlfriends reminded me that all Curvy sections are not created equal, so if you are looking for larger sizes that don't skimp on being stylish, sexy, cool, or comfy – check these out:

1. **Torrid**
2. **Ashley Stewart**
3. **Dia** (shop.dia.com)
4. **Cuup**
5. **Avenue**
6. **June and Evie** (juneandevie.com)
7. **Swimsuits for All** (swimsuitsforall.com)

Premium Outlet Stores

Another opportunity to snatch affordable luxury can be found at premium outlet stores. Any luxury brand with an outlet allows you to look great on a budget—Saks Fifth Avenue, Coach, and Neiman Marcus, for example, are places where you can find deals and still take advantage of affordable prices depending on the location and season. If there is a store that you love that seems out of your budget, always check and see if they have an outlet within driving distance of you.

Disclaimer: This is not an exhaustive list. Remember that the stores and brands we mentioned are popular in the regions we cover, the mid-Atlantic and southern areas of the United States. Please let us know which ones we still need to include by messaging us on social media or emailing me at info@rainahdavis.com! We are glad to create more editions to keep the information relevant, and we appreciate your help in doing so!

Ultimately, this guide lets you determine which brands are within your budget and gives you the tools you need to secure them. Now, it's YOUR turn to shop! Regardless of which brands you purchase, rest assured you'll get a combination of style and quality. As a woman working towards achieving the best in life, your wardrobe cannot get left behind. It's time to look luxurious on a budget. So, go out there and do it. Happy shopping!

CHAPTER 3:

Build Your Wardrobe

While this is one of the book's shorter chapters, it doesn't make it less vital. Once you have established a clear budget and are ready to go shopping, there are three essential closet needs that will help you win the wardrobe war: classics, trend items, and signature items.

Classics are clothes that will never go out of style and have been popular throughout fashion history. These classic colors, patterns, and silhouettes should be the skeleton of your wardrobe—the main features or the nuts and bolts. Tori shares the importance of these items in our wardrobe!

Tori Talks Fashion

Classics are a lifeline. With every client I have, I always ask them if they have certain classic pieces: a black blazer, a black dress, a white button-up, an essential trench coat, a great pair of jeans, etc. Classic pieces always stay in style. They always come in handy, and they're easily incorporated with trends and signature styles. Another thing to consider with classics is color selection. Neutral colors like black, white, navy, gray, or beige are commonly used when pairing garments.

Trends are a great way to keep your wardrobe updated without going overboard. I would choose less expensive trend items because they don't always stay in style. You don't want to waste your money on a trendy luxury item that may not be popular next season. Trends can easily be attained by buying accessories or incorporating fun colors with your newly purged wardrobe.

Signature-style items always make you feel your best. These can include any classic items you think are well incorporated with your trend items. I love monochromatic dressing, where you dress head to toe in one shade or tone. Then, I infuse pieces to keep my look updated. I have found that classic pieces like blazers, trench coats, white button-ups, and a great pair of jeans have become my signature style. Simple statement pieces with flair have been my go-to.

Similarly, Rainah shared that patterned tights are her signature item. She loves their comfort and versatility, and while they may have started as a trend, she incorporated them into her signature item.

Some college student-athletes signature items include a brightly colored athletic shoe, a super funky sports bra, or a uniquely designed baseball cap. Others may lean into bold, bulky jewelry or statement pieces. Whatever it is, when you determine what your items are, rock them like nobody's business! Nothing makes you walk into a room and own it, like deciding your unique signature items.

Besos, Tori

CHAPTER 4

Your Best Fit—Wardrobe Specialties

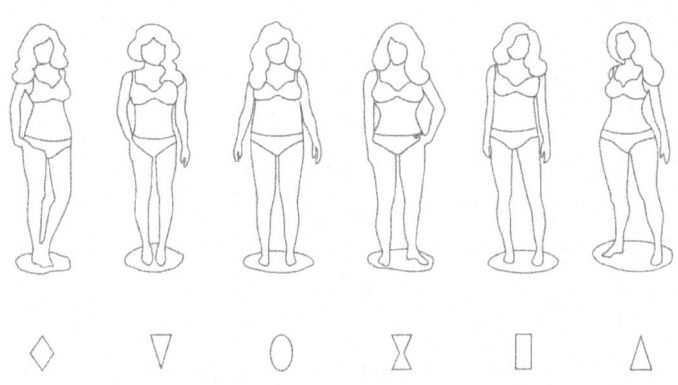

Diamond • Inverted Triangle • Oval • Hourglass • Rectangle • Triangle
(body shapes left to right)

Discover the Fashion That Works for Your Body

Have you ever ordered a dress online, and when you put it on, you realized you didn't look like the model who originally wore it? I'm not talking about stores that sell poor-quality clothing. On the contrary, the same outfit can look flattering on someone else. This unfortunate occurrence usually happens when an item is not a good fit for our specific body type or shape.

Before we dive into the three main types, I want to introduce you to some and provide a refresher for others: an overview of body shapes. Understanding your body's type and shape will help you make fashion selections that accentuate your unique features. While researching all the types, I found a host of stylists, bloggers, and fashionistas who give specific suggestions for every body type. You can see the links for each article referenced in the References section after the book. The main objective is to briefly introduce each type to help you learn how to accentuate your best features!

Let's be honest: we all look different. The same clothing items cannot work for all of us. However, we can still look good despite our physical differences. The secret lies in knowing your body type and dressing it well. This guide will cover the different body types to help you figure out where you fall and how to flatter your body shape best. Believe me; every type has positives; the key is to work with what your mama gave you! Our favorite stylist gives us tips to keep in mind as we head into this chapter.

Tori Talks Fashion

Dressing for your body type is critical and crucial! I have seen such a remarkable difference in my client's confidence when we apply customized looks based strictly on their body type and build. As you learn about the ideal looks for your shape and size, a personal stylist can help you achieve your desired look. Don't be afraid to seek help; I tell my petite and curvy ladies to avoid oversized styles. Tailored looks accentuate the curves and make you incredible! I encourage petite ladies to try monochromatic looks because wearing one color from head to toe will make you look taller and leaner when they are shorter. Remember, your favorite stylists and influencers often share tips that will blow your mind. Let this be the first stop on your wardrobe journey. Keep learning!

Besos, Tori!

The Body Shape Breakdown

1. The Diamond Body Shape

Ladies with this silhouette often have broader hips than shoulders, slender limbs, and a small bust.

Key Features:
- Average or wide hips
- Undefined waist
- Small bust
- Narrow shoulders
- Slender yet shapely legs

International personal stylist service *Lookiero* suggests that A-line, belted, or flared dresses best-fit diamond body shapes because they accentuate the upper torso and draw the eyes to the waist.

2. The Inverted Triangle Shape

Women with an inverted triangle shape have top-heavy figures with an undefined waistline. These ladies' shoulders are broader than their hips, with typically long and slender legs.

Key Features:

- Minimal waist definition
- Broad shoulders wider than hips
- Heavy bust
- Long, slender legs

The Concept Wardrobe suggests that jumpsuits and playsuits are girl's best friends if they are an inverted triangle because their broader shoulders let the garments fall nicely down their silhouette.

3. The Oval (Apple) Shape

Women with the oval/apple shape have a larger midsection and chest area. The shoulders and hips are proportional, while the waist is not very defined and tends to be wider than the hips.

Key Features:
- Heavy bust
- Fuller midsection
- Narrow hips
- Undefined waistline

Global stylists at *Lookiero* suggest going for straight-cut, empire waists, and asymmetric lines dresses. Also, this type looks fabulous in boot cut, wide-leg, and palazzo trousers, creating a curvier shape. Last, this body shape looks best in garments that create vertical lines (which lengthen their silhouettes), items with flowy fabrics, and solid colors rather than busy prints.

4. The Hourglass (Figure 8) Shape

The classic hourglass has an equally distributed figure and a well-defined waist. The bust and hip measurements are roughly equal, and the legs are in proportion with the upper body.

Key Features:

- Shoulders are usually rounded, from delicate to broad in size
- Bust size is medium to full and proportionate to the lower body curves
- A defined, sharp waist
- Curvy hipline
- Leg length is proportional to the overall length of the body

We love the Bella Ella Boutique's suggestions for the hourglass shapes. They recommend accentuating the natural waistline with high-waisted styles or belts, dresses that hug curves like peplum, paneled waist and wrap dresses, skirts like A-line and pencil skirts, and accessorizing with statement jewelry.

5. The Rectangle Shape

The rectangle shape has a well-balanced figure with no defined waistline. The shoulder, bust, and hip measurements are roughly equal, and the legs are in proportion with the upper body.

Key Features:

- Bust, hips, and shoulders all have similar widths
- Long legs and minimal curve to the entire silhouette
- Vertical length and lean look
- Minimal waist definition or no defined waist
- Smaller bust and butt

One of the most comprehensive guides for this body type was created by Gabrielle Arruda (remember all research for this section is listed in the references so that you can read the full articles). On her site, she details the best looks for this type, even down to the best sleeve types! As an overview, this body type looks best when wearing soft, flowy tops and playing with curvy necklines. She suggests large collars, ruffles, plunging V-necks, scoop tops, sweetheart-shaped blouses, turtlenecks, and mandarin collars.

Additionally, this type looks best when you break up the silhouette horizontally from top to bottom on both your top and bottom halves. It is best to use volume in the right areas; for example–with your bottom half, opt for silhouettes that gently flare out, and for flair, add color to the top half of your body. Gabrielle also has illustrations if you are unfamiliar with some of these styles!

6. The Triangle (Pear) Shape

The classic triangle shape has a bottom-heavy figure and a slim upper body. The hip measurements are larger than the shoulders, and the legs are in proportion with the upper body.

Key Features:

- A-shape silhouette
- Medium to small in height
- Shoulders are slimmer compared to the hips
- Pronounced waistline
- Delicate bust
- Defined hips that are wider than the shoulders

Style DNA recommends tops that visually broaden your shoulder line because they add dimension to the upper body. Examples are blouses with shoulder pads, eye-catching prints, off-shoulder, high necklines, and lots of color and details. Bottoms that are fitted and straight cuts show off this type's naturally curvy lower body. Again, sleeves matter; with this body type, petal, cap, flutter, and batwing, all are winners! You can read more of our research in the Reference section.

This chapter teaches you to select the best garments to activate your radiant beauty and confidence. If you want to look different, get in shape, or change some features at any point in your journey, we applaud that, too! Just be sure to love your body while working for the body you want. Please continue reading to learn more about body types and additional ways to look our absolute best!

Common Body Types

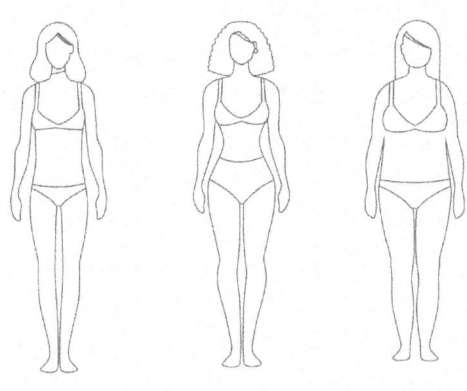

Ectomorphs • Mesomorphs • Endomorphs
(body types left to right)

There are three main body types: ectomorphs, mesomorphs, and endomorphs. Do you know which one you are? If not, let's find out!

1. Ectomorphs

Ectomorphs are people with slender frames and lean bodies. They have narrow hips, small waists, and muscles, not to mention long arms and legs.

Ectomorphs have a fast metabolism, which means their bodies burn calories rapidly. Therefore, it's hard for them to have a lot of body fat, no matter how much or frequently they eat. If people always tell you you look like a model, this is your body type. To dress as an ectomorph, please continue reading.

Tops: Start by getting a proper-fitting bra. A well-fitted bra will enhance your posture, boost confidence, and improve your outfit. This tip applies to all body types. You should also consider embracing halter neck tops, as they immediately make you look stylish without appearing like you are trying too hard. They also give your upper body more volume, making you look more attractive.

Tops that make your bust area look fuller include those with printed tops or ruffles. Coats and blazers accentuate your small waist. You can achieve this by adding a belt or button around your waist to show your figure.

Bright-colored blouses and shirts also make you look good. Their effect is enhanced further when your bottom is a contrasting color. As an ectomorph, you want to avoid baggy clothes because they hide your shape and make you look unflattering. Also, low necks make you look like you have a smaller bust, so they're not the best for you unless you're wearing a push-up bra to add volume to your chest.

Bottoms: Flared trousers will make your legs look even longer and give your bottom a great shape. These can be flared from your knee downwards or even from your waist. When paired with wedges or a small heel, you'll look amazing.

You can also wear fitted bottoms (jeans, leggings, or regular trousers) that hug your body. When paired with boots or heels, a knee-length dress or pencil skirt accentuates your body shape. Another type of skirt you should consider is the A-line skirt because it flatters your body—the more details it has, the better.

2. Mesomorphs

Mesomorphs are muscular and have a moderate-sized physique. They look athletic with broad shoulders, medium-sized busts, and hips. Their waists are smaller, and their arms and legs look strong. It is easy for mesomorphs to build muscle and gain or lose weight because they have an efficient metabolism. Here are some tips on how to dress as a mesomorph.

Tops: Consider stocking up on slim-fit shirts or clothes that stretch to give you a flattering silhouette without being too tight or loose. Loose clothes don't do your curvy shape justice, so stay away from those. If your jackets are baggy, you can take them to the tailor to remove any unnecessary material around your waist. This alteration will make your shape more visible.

Since you have broader shoulders and a smaller waist, forming a 'V' shape, shirts with this shape best accentuate your form. You can pair the 'V' shirt with straight-leg pants to complete the look. Jeans and T-shirts will also flatter your body.

It would be best to opt for clothing with vertical lines, not horizontal ones. Horizontal lines make you appear bigger than you are. Anything that makes your shoulders look broader is a no-no. Examples of these are sleeveless tops and padded jackets. Tops with soft prints are great for you because they don't add volume around your torso area and remove some of the attention from your bust area (if this is what you want). Since you have a sizable bust, you don't need bras with extra padding because these add volume to your chest area.

Bottoms: Shorts will look great on you since your legs (and sometimes your butt) are toned. Short and tight clothing will generally enhance your beauty. How short you want to go depends on your comfort zone.

Straight-leg pants will flatter your shape, especially with the tops discussed above (such as the 'V' shirts). Get pants that hug your waist and/or hip area but are loose at the ankle. They give off a slight flare at the bottom. Think along the lines of bootcut trousers.

If you wear bold colors or patterns at the top, you can balance them with lighter shades and prints at the bottom. You have an excellent shape for dresses, so don't be scared to put them on. Bodycon and wrap dresses would look stunning because they accentuate your waist and highlight your curves.

3. Endomorphs

Endomorphs are generally curvy because their slow metabolism makes it easier for them to gain weight quickly but lose it slowly. So, they have heavier busts, wider hips, and are rounder. How to dress as an endomorph:

Tops: A low scoop is an excellent opportunity to show your fantastic bust. If you feel your bust is too big and want to cover it or tone it down, tops with high cuts or neutral-colored ones will do the trick. Vertical lines make you appear leaner, so they're great for you. Horizontal lines do the opposite, so avoid them if you can. Shirts that draw too much attention to your chest will not look flattering. Examples are those with big pictures or phrases or oversized graphic prints.

Bottoms: Since you have a wider waist, you need bottoms that flow with your shape. Therefore, there are better options than dresses or pants that hold your waist too tightly. Clothing with repeat prints will also look flattering on you. Just make sure it's your size and not loose-fitting because that will make you look bigger.

Classic clothing will always look great on you. Examples include monochromatic outfits or those with subtle patterns. Dark colors flatter you the most. Clothes with pockets and belts also make you appear bigger. If you want to dress down, try wearing a long cardigan with skinny jeans or leggings. You could also wear a maxi skirt over slim-fitting pants or shorts to add shape.

The good news is that there are incredible clothing items for each type. All you need to do is embrace your body type, wear clothes that flatter you, and add confidence! Again, I urge you not to compare yourself to anyone else. If you are not where you want to be physically, I encourage you to love the body you have and work for the body you want! You can change your diet and nutrition, or if your doctor approves, you can do medical weight loss or surgery. There are several ways to achieve the look you want. In the meantime, please dress the body you have (right now) in a way that makes you look and feel like the rockstar you are!

Also, remember chapter one, where we attacked the closet? This new information may cause you to go back and do a second round. Why? Now you know the clothes that flatter you the most and can make room for them by applying these few things:

1. **Purge (part two)**: get rid of clothes that are taking up space and are not flattering to your body type. Purging and decluttering will create space for items that elevate and enhance your appearance.

2. **Begin the wardrobe rebuild/remix**: now that you know what to shop for and have created space for these clothing items, it's time to start building your wardrobe. Invest in the pieces recommended in this article, depending on your body type. Remember, you can also buy classics (they never go out of style) and a couple of trends you love and may want to make a part of your signature style.

For example, being from North Carolina, I embraced patterned tights during winter, and they became part of my signature items because of their comfort and versatility. Fall and winter were often cool in the morning and warmer in the afternoon, so these were perfect for my dressier looks. Although Tori and I have already mentioned signature looks a few times, we will get into that more in Chapter 6.

Finally, be patient with your style journey. Don't blow your budget! I cannot stress this enough. Building an ideal wardrobe that compliments your body type will not happen in a day. Initially, you can remix your current wardrobe with new items as you obtain them. We are on a marathon, not a sprint; stay on the path, and it will be worth it! In the meantime, let's talk about other items that help you find a great fit.

Body Shapers

Shapewear is a closet staple that several women continue to achieve. It can become an essential component of any woman's wardrobe because it is the foundation for all her other outfits. The best part is that you can quickly put it on without worrying about it conflicting with any sense of fashion. Continue reading about why shapewear is an essential staple in your closet and whether you should wear it for a big event or an easygoing hang out with your friends.

Contrary to a one-time look, shapewear is a long-term investment that should be worn regularly to shape and contour your body, giving you the most control under your clothes for a body-sculpting impact. The best shapewear should be invisible and not bulge or show line hints under clothing. Shapewear is available in various styles to address body parts and areas of concern, including bodysuits, girdles, abdomen binders, corsets, and brassieres. It is versatile and can be worn with any outfit to contour your figure seamlessly. You'll feel more confident going out if you look good.

Shapewear is a great way to fit into your favorite clothes, including cocktail dresses, evening party attire, and work clothes. It is the ideal go-to option whether attending a party or going to the office. You don't have to wear anything that will drastically alter your figure. Instead, it's about boosting your silhouette; shapewear works like a charm. Shapewear is accessible for almost every body area, including the waist, belly, abdomen, hips, and thighs. Every woman must understand her ace of spades when finding the right spot.

Here are a few examples:

1. **Tummy shapewear**: shows off an enviably toned figure while promising a waistband that won't roll down. It conceals tummy fat and does not have any zippers or hooks. Because of its hydrofoil fiber knit lining, this shapewear delivers smooth, ultimate comfort and seamless edges.

2. **Classic desk spin-on—high waist shapewear**: shapewear with a high waist covers your thighs and extends higher than or equal to your torso, usually ending just below the bust. It effectively achieves a slimmer feminine appearance by narrowing the waistline. In addition, high waist shapewear is ideal for creating smooth bulges that fit like a second skin.

3. **Thigh shapewear with sculptural shaping**: This shapewear that uses specific shapewear is the key to giving the illusion of slimmer thighs. It focuses on your thighs, causing them to look thinner and more toned. And the best part is that it is entirely undetectable beneath your clothing! That's a good bang for your buck!

4. **Corsets included—full body shaper**: This elongated body shaper is excellent for an all-around solution. Whether you aim to slim your silhouette or dramatically conceal unwanted bumps, full-body shapers will contour your body type whenever you look in the mirror. It shapes your thighs, defines your waist, lifts your bust, and even serves as a comfortable option for a bra.

Regardless of type, shapewear provides an excellent foundation for clothing to drape correctly and allows you to bring every outfit perfectly. If you don't already have one and don't like how you look in some garments, I suggest you purchase one to help you fit into any clothing!

Undergarment Options

Understandably, some people have different aims for their garments or undergarments. However, to choose the best things for you, you must first determine what you desire those things to do. Whether you want to be more sexy or comfortable, different undergarments are vital to your outfit's appearance. Here are our top brands of undergarments:

- *Classic Briefs*: designed to provide complete coverage. They have full-back low-leg openings, and they (finally) come up high just on the belly. We used to call these "granny panties," but they've been making a comeback in recent years.

- *Bikinis*: have a low hip cut and a high cut on the leg. They provide minimal to moderate back coverage. Some demonstrate the top of the backside and plenty of cheek, while others offer more protection. String bikinis are also popular, with the sides supplanted by thin fabric or simply elastic. Bikinis are the most popular type of underwear. However, they are not suitable for most body types.

- **High-length briefs**: a version of the classic brief with the same high waist and full back but with a much larger leg opening.
- **Hipsters** is another classic brief variant with the same low leg openings and a full-back as the classic but with a lower rise (think bikini meets the classic brief).
- **Boyshorts** resemble the low-rise shorts worn by volleyball players. They have very low leg openings, complete coverage in the back, and are typically low to mid-rise in height.
- **Thongs** are last but not least, but kind of least—no pun intended! These undergarments have a low to high rise, varying amounts of side coverage, and no back coverage. This option is great when you wear very fitted clothing and want to avoid showing panty lines. If you oppose them, "pantyhose" is another option.

Remember, depending on your comfort level and desired goal, the type you choose will depend a lot on your desired outcome. We do not cover bras here, but the most crucial thing about bras is wearing the correct size. I know times are different, but you can go to your local department store lingerie department and get fitted. If that makes you uncomfortable, you can also search for "home bra fitting" on YouTube, and several videos will pop up (some of them are by popular retailers).

Lastly, when it comes to your look, we suggest that after you know your size, you purchase a strapless bra, adjustable strap bra, and nipple covers to prepare you for evening gowns, specialty tops, and blouses. This a good segue into another garment worn close to the body: your bathing suit.

Beach Ready:
Your Best Bathing Suit Fits

With these tips, you can choose the ideal bathing suit to flatter your figure and make you look stunning. Below, you will find various body types and careful instructions on how to select the proper suit. Before we check in with our favorite personal stylist, I can't emphasize enough that we are all beautiful in our uniqueness. So, let's get started!

Tori Talks Fashion

Keep this in mind: bathing suits can be tricky. However, knowing your body type will also help with that. Another cheat code that I give my ladies is getting a bathing suit with support like built-in bras and even compression features that smooth out any imperfections you think you may have without suffocating you! We share more tips below!

Besos, Tori

Finding Your Swim Suit Fit

A **large chest** requires support, but finding bra-like support can be difficult. To provide support and lift, look for underwire or molded cups. You're in luck if you can find a swimsuit with your cup sizes like a regular bra! Also, halter tops and adjustable straps will help keep any wardrobe mishaps at bay.

Those with large chests believe that their petite peer equivalents have it easier, but that does not mean that petite girls don't have challenges finding the perfect suit. Padding and push-up tops will draw attention to your top or to those with a **small chest**.

If you have curvy thighs and hips and a smaller top, you are a **pear shape**. Enhance your chest with a plunging neckline and an eye-catching top to draw the eye away from your lower half. Skirted bottoms disguise the thickness of the thighs (if you are shy). Forego the boy's short bottoms because unless they fit just right, they can be less flattering to the lower half.

Even though they don't have to complain about balancing proportions, **athletic builds** face many choices regarding swimwear. Choose a monokini to create curves; this aesthetic will end things in straight lines. High-leg bottoms also are helpful because they highlight toned legs. Feel free to reach for feminine frills in bikinis and avoid bandeaus even though they create straight lines across the chest.

A **curvy** figure does not imply size. Curvy women come in all shapes and sizes, but they all have one thing in common: a balanced upper and half with a defined waistline. Fortunately, this body type can wear almost any kind of swimsuit. A balconette top with high-waisted bottoms will also provide support while drawing attention to your tiny waist. Consider retro bombshells like Bettie Page and Marilyn Monroe when shopping for swimsuits.

If you're worried about showing off your stomach, plenty of bathing suit choices are both flattering and fabulous. The one-piece is a classic, and the designs have gotten cuter in recent years. High-waisted bottoms are enjoyable because they allow you to wear whatever top you want while **concealing your midsection**. Tankinis are an excellent alternative to one-piece swimsuits due to their full-coverage two-piece that is easier to remove when you must use the restroom.

Wardrobe Cheat Codes:
Making Every Item Look Its Best

One of the most overlooked hacks to crafting and rocking a killer outfit is having it tailored or altered. Continue reading for more details on how to achieve this look properly.

Tailoring/alterations can transform the entire wardrobe as well as the way you feel in your clothes. Tailoring can accentuate, elongate, help you appear taller and slimmer, or even help you minimize definite areas to make the optimum fit in your favorite pieces. However, it is an additional investment that you must be willing to make. We highly recommend you make the sacrifice at least during three scenarios:

1. **Clothing for special occasions:** prom, homecoming, wedding ceremonies, or even a business meeting—your clothing should make a great impression on your most important occasions. Tailoring can turn your garments into pieces you'll be able to wear for years to come, garments that can evolve with fashion trends and a transition among different potential fits.

Knowing your clothing items fit you perfectly gives you the confidence to face any occasion.

2. **Favorite clothes:** may include your favorite pair of jeans. What about that favorite work suit that never fits correctly for you? Tailoring can help you get more wear out of your favorite clothes. Alterations also enable you to tailor the fit of your favorite garments to your specific needs over time.

3. **New clothes,** especially when they are expensive and you aim to dress them up for a long time, are better invested in tailoring. Tailoring enables you to attain the perfect fit in your clothing while also making sure that your clothing can develop with you for years to come. In addition, alterations will allow you to continue wearing your expensive items even if your measurements or body changes.

The benefit of tailored clothing is that it is made to last. Therefore, altering your clothing can assist you with fast fashion by selecting an elevated, tailor-made garment from specialists with years of experience. In addition, sometimes changing a more expensive piece of clothing to a better fit can help you receive more wear out of it by lowering the likelihood of requiring repairs—a wise investment.

Finally, tailoring provides sophistication and specialization that off-the-rack clothing does not. For example, with tailoring, you can select cuts and styles, pleats as well as darts, and many other fully customizable options that add stuff uniquely "you" to your clothing or ensemble.

Wardrobe Tools

Wardrobe tools to keep on hand include a clothing care kit of a few basic things that can go a long way:

1. **Lint rollers**: sticky lint rollers only cost a few dollars and are the quickest way to eliminate hair, lint, and dust. Use on any fabric as often as needed or if the item has been sitting unworn for an extended period and might be dusty.

2. **Needle and thread**: if you need basic sewing skills, you can learn how to sew a button or mend a hole from YouTube videos. Or if you have a friend who can sew a button, it will only take them

a few minutes to show you. Chances are they would rather teach you than sew it for you!

3. **Lint remover:** these can be either a small comb or an electric device to remove lint balls from sweaters that make them look worn out. This small device helps keep your clothes in good shape for longer.

4. **Steamers** are excellent tools that help your wardrobe look sharp and wrinkle-free. Steamers are great for a busy woman who wants to look her best. Steaming has many benefits:

   - Works on delicate fabrics like wool and silk without getting shiny spots that you might get from an iron.
   - Safe on synthetic fabrics like polyester that can melt under the high heat of an iron.
   - Steamers specifically take up less space than an ironing board.

5. **Irons** are good if you need to press something flat or in a particular direction, such as collars, cuffs, or pintucks. If you have a blouse that you want crisp, an iron is the best for this. However, steamers are faster and easier if you want to get

creases out of tops, pants, and trousers. Steaming is often the safest for blazers, jackets, and dresses, as you don't need a press cloth to cover delicate fabrics. It's also easier to navigate sleeves as you won't have to worry about creasing fabric on the other side of your ironing.

Fabric Selections That Fit Your Life

Choosing the suitable fabrics that work for you and your lifestyle is essential to wardrobe building. There are a few tips to consider. For example, when adding to your wardrobe, it's a good idea to be mindful of the fabrics you choose and your lifestyle. For example, life can get messy and busy if you have young kids. Fabrics that wash easily make life go a little smoother.

Take a moment to look at the care label on clothing before buying if you need easy-to-wash and dry clothing. Dark or patterned fabrics also hide stains better if this concerns you.

Easy care fabric selections help you avoid dry-clean-only clothing if it doesn't fit your lifestyle. Some items, like a silk blouse, can be hand-washed and hung to dry instead of dry-cleaned, but you might have better options. Jackets and coats are an exception—these typically are dry-clean only. Still, they don't usually have to be cleaned that often. Consider spot cleaning with a damp cloth and hanging in fresh air to cut down on dry cleaning.

To help your clothes last as long as possible, follow these steps:

1. Close zippers before washing to help prevent damage to the zipper. This process prevents the zipper from snagging other items in the wash.
2. Do pay attention to the care instructions.
3. Don't wash garments any more than necessary.
4. Cold water helps prevent the shrinking of fabrics and can lessen the amount of dye that bleeds from fabric.
5. Turn jeans inside out to prevent color bleeding.
6. Always wash dark colors together.
7. Hang cotton clothes to dry to prevent shrinking.

Additionally, different types of fabrics have specific care needs. Natural fibers are made from natural materials, and synthetic fibers are man-made. Some will fit into your lifestyle better than others. Here are some of the most common fabrics for clothing and their pros and cons.

Synthetic fabrics include:

- Polyester
- Nylon
- Rayon
- Elastane
- Performance fabrics (fabrics for athletic wear, waterproof fabrics, etc.)
- Acrylic

Pros:

- Typically, it is cheaper than most natural fabrics.
- They don't usually wrinkle as easily as natural fibers.
- Easy to machine wash, can generally go in the dryer (always check)
- Don't tend to shrink in the wash.

Cons:

- Synthetic fibers can melt if the iron heat is too high.

- Synthetic fibers are less breathable, which increases sweat
- Synthetic fibers tend to wear out faster than natural fabrics

Particularly polyester (found in tops, trousers, dresses, etc.) and acrylic (often found in knit sweaters and is prone to pilling)

Natural fibers include:

- Cotton
- Linen
- Silk
- Wool

Pros:

- Breathable: Natural fibers are a much better choice for warmer climates and seasons than synthetic fabrics.
- Longer lasting: Natural fibers are less prone to pilling than most synthetic fibers and stay looking new and in good condition longer.

Cons:

- Prone to shrinking in heat, particularly cotton and wool. It is wise to hang cotton clothing to dry instead of putting it in the dryer. Never put wool in the dryer, and only wash cold.
- Natural fibers wrinkle easily, especially linen.
- Linen and wool usually cost more than synthetic fabrics.

In general, synthetic fabrics cost less upfront and are easier to care for, but they wear out quickly. Synthetic fibers may work for you if you are watching your budget and like clothes that are easy to wash and wear, as there typically is less shrinkage or special care instructions.

Natural fibers cost a bit more and need a bit more care. However, this is often worth it as the fabrics stay in good condition longer and are more breathable than synthetic fabrics. Natural fabrics are a better choice if you are looking for quality pieces that you want to last a long time. If you are getting something you know you will only wear a few times, choosing a synthetic fabric can help cut costs.

Specialty fabrics while delicate fabrics such as silk can be worn regularly, they might not fit into your lifestyle in terms of the extra care of this fabric. Wool can also be tricky to care for; it is often dry-cleaned. Again, lots of consideration depending on your budget and lifestyle.

Fabric blends can offer the best of both worlds: they are made from a mix of materials—for example, a blouse that is 70% cotton and 30% polyester. If you can find wool/cotton blend fabric or silk/cotton blend fabric, these are often slightly more practical choices than the 100% wool or silk versions. Cotton/polyester blend fabric can also be a good choice if you want a good fabric that is less prone to shrinking and wrinkling than 100% cotton, especially for blouses.

This chapter was stuffed with a lot of information. Instead of trying to remember it all, we suggest you use it as a reference guide.

CHAPTER 5:

The Joy of Dressing—
Accents & Accessories

Before we break down all the types of accessories, Tori has shared her thoughts with us below!

Tori Talks Fashion

Accessories, accessories, accessories! Accessories can make or break an entire look. It's essential to have great accessories in your wardrobe. Accessories can change the look from day to night. I would start out with a nude shoe, a black shoe, and a white sneaker. Then, maybe choose any pop-of-color shoe to add some spice and personality.

Likewise, I personally love chunky, oversized pieces of jewelry, but I also have a simple side. A few bold accessories can be easily added to a simple white T-shirt and black pants to make it look like this wow statement outfit.

Hats are also a game-changer for me. They instantly change the mood of an outfit and sometimes are showstoppers. My secret solution to a bad hair day is a great hat! What started out as a simple fix can end up making the outfit!

In this chapter, we discuss signature style more deeply. For me, hats have become a signature style. If a hat is your signature style, this is an area where you can invest in something more expensive so that it will last longer. Overall, accessories are a perfect way to make outfits effortless. What you wear should be an extension of the best you.

Besos, Tori

Tori already told us that hats and shoes are critical pieces for our accessory game. Let's dissect this even more. First, have you ever looked at your outfit in the mirror and felt like something was missing? Well, I've been there more times than you can imagine. One trick I learned over the years is that accessorizing is one of the most important parts of looking good, stylish, and put together.

A great selection of timeless accessories can completely change an outfit and take it to a whole new level. Most women agree that accessories complement your outfits if they are used in the right way.

Many women don't wear accessories out of habit or because they do not understand how important they are; while it's okay for everyone to be comfortable in whatever they choose to wear, some accessories are a must-have. Every woman needs a stack of basic accessories that can add sass to any outfit, from trendy bags and classic belts to beautiful jewelry. So, are you ready to take your look from drab to glam but are unsure where to begin? No worries! This chapter covers the basics of accessorizing and explains how to accentuate any outfit with just a few pieces.

Shoes:
Never Underestimate the Power of the Right Pair of Shoes

It is always tempting to purchase the latest trending pair of shoes that catches your eye. You even promise yourself that you will wear the shoes before they go out of style this time. Eventually, you only wear the shoes twice and toss them in your closet. The next thing you know, you begin to feel you do not have any classic shoes that suit most of your outfits.

It is very easy to fall deep into the trap of buying trend-driven shoes and forget the long game. So, read below for a few shoe types that are important for every woman.

1. **Ballerina flats** are one of the most versatile shoes because they can go with virtually any look. It doesn't matter if you wear a skinny dress, skirt, shorts, or a dress; wearing a pair of solid-colored ballerina flats will give your outfits a finished look.

2. **Pumps** are pairs of heels that are essential for every woman. Whether you are all about heels or you avoid them, a pair of pencil-heeled pumps is a must-have. Pumps are typically made of suede material or patent leather; however, they look classy and will improve your look regardless of the occasion. I also keep a comfy pair for in-person office meetings, consultations, job/media interviews, business trips, dressy church outfits (which happens less and less), and speaking engagements, when appropriate.

3. **Ankle strap heels**–if you wish to make a statement at an event, there is no better way to do this than to storm the place dressed gorgeously and wearing strappy heels. The heels on these shoes will surely bring out your feminine, confident, and fierce side. A classic strap heel is a must-have for dressy looks and special occasions. These shoes can glam up any outfit with minimal effort from you.

4. **Flip-flops/Crocs and other slip-on** shoes are convenient, easy to wear, and a must-have for every woman. They are readily available in

vibrant colors and patterns and are very comfortable. If you have errands to run or are headed to the beach, having a pair of flip-flops is your best bet. Over time, you should invest in ones with support. Crocs, Birkenstocks, and other orthopedic/athletic versions are much safer as we age.

5. **Sneakers** have been trendy for a long time; from everyday looks to evening events, they've got you covered. You can pair sneakers with almost anything; a pair of sneakers gives you a cool, confident, and chic vibe. So, get yourself a good, top-quality pair and flip your look without hassle. You can also switch from shoes that look like Keds to Jordans or wedge-like sneakers. Sneakers like these give a slight edge to your athleisure looks and transform your outfit for a last-minute date night with your boo, a church event (where you want to be cute but not so cool that you can't move around) or a spontaneous night out with the girls! However, let's be clear; "style" sneakers should not replace the *Adidas, Nike, Puma, New Balance, or Brooks* shoes you use for training,

running, yoga, cardio, and other fitness goals. Depending on your preferences, you may opt for a Converse or Vann for casual looks and errands.

6. **Boots** are another pair of shoes you need, especially on cold days or days you want to give your look a little razzle-dazzle, spice, or kick! Boots will also give your outfit a chic look and strike that perfect finish. There are many kinds of boots that you can pick based on your preference and personal taste. UGGs, Timberlands, riding boots, knee-highs, rainboots, ankle-length boots, western-styled cowboy boots, wedges, stiletto heels, kitten heels, and combat boots are popular choices ranging from stylish to practical.

7. **Flat sandals** are a must-have addition for summer and spring. Sandals will go perfectly with any dress, jeans, and even shorts. In addition, if you love going to a beach destination, you must have at least a pair of flat sandals in your collection. So, pick a pair today for casual everyday chores and another for more formal occasions.

Fall Favorites:
Chic Ways to Work Your Scarf

You can wear your favorite scarf and still look chic in different ways. Here are a few you can try out:

1. **Loose knot**: A loose knot works well with breezier outfits, especially on warm days, so your scarf does not hug too tight or overheat your throat. How do you make a loose knot? You fold the scarf in half, drape it over your neck, take both loose ends of your scarf, and thread them through the open loop created, tugging the loose ends slightly to make a knot.

2. **The drape look:** Another way to wear your scarf is to drape it over the back of your neck, leaving the two ends to hang down to frame your body. You can try this method over a t-shirt to display the scarf's beauty and length.

3. Another smart way to wear a scarf is to try the **square scarf**. Simply fold the square scarf in half at the content and place it on your chest. Then, you can grab both ends and wrap them around

your neck. This simple style works well with a button-down shirt and blazer.

4. **The double knot**: First, hold the center of your scarf at your chest, take the left end of the scarf, and place it around your neck and right shoulder. Then, repeat the same step with the left shoulder. This will make a 'U' shape from the center of the scarf and at your chest. Next, twist the 'U' to become the figure eight, thread the left side through one hole, and repeat with the right side. Finally, tighten it according to your level of comfort and tuck it into your coat. When you are done, it should look like challah dough; a style that is beautiful under a peacoat.

5. **A low-hanging knot:** Having a larger scarf is an opportunity to try different styles and find your favorite way of wearing it. In addition, you can change your look by hanging your scarf around your neck and making a low-hanging knot out of the longer ends.

6. **Wear it like a shawl**: Another way to change your look with a scarf is to drape a wide and long scarf over your shoulders and hold it with a fashionable

belt around your waist. The belt will create sleeves, and your scarf will look like a shawl.

Hold Up! Don't Forget About Belts

Having a collection of belts to match every outfit is a game-changer. Belts can instantly transform your look, and you can style them with dresses, pants, and oversized T-shirts. Wearing belts is another way to improve your looks, and here are the different types of belts a woman should have in her closet:

- **Classic leather belt**—Every lady needs at least one clean, classic **leather belt** in her closet. This belt is made of leather and is one of the most common belts in most closets. It is an essential female accessory that never goes out of style and is something to hold on to during winter, fall, summer, and spring. The leather belt is a classic must-have for every woman with style.
- **Studded belt**—A studded belt can spice up your look and add glitz to your outfit. You can wear studded belts on your dress or pants,

remembering to tuck half your blouse to show off this incredible and eccentric piece. A studded belt is an eye-catching accessory that will benefit every woman's wardrobe.

- **Pearl waist belt**—Feeling fancy? Many women love pairing their looks with earrings and necklaces, so why not add a **pearl waist belt** to them? A pearl waist belt will look perfect with a long gown for a party, date night, or night out with the girls. Having an elegant pearl in the middle of a leather belt with beautiful designs and other elements will be one of the most eye-catching accessories for women.

- **Skinny belts**—These belts look perfect when paired with a straight dress or high-waist jeans. You can also wear skinny belts daily, as they give even the simplest outfit a finished and luxurious look.

- **Braided belts** are a go-to for vintage and classic looks. We know that giving an outfit a finishing touch can really make or break your look. So, a **braided belt** will be cool and chic to add to any dress, especially when you want to give a bold fashion impression. You can fit the braided belt perfectly on your hips or upper waist. Braided belts are a perfect accent to style your tops and dresses.

Bling, Rings, & More: Your Jewelry Box

Finding your style is a lifelong journey. It's much easier if you understand your preferences and have clothes to help you create your unique look. When you do, you'll be out the door at the right time every day.

However, no outfit is complete without adding the right accessories to match. It doesn't matter if you attend an official, formal, professional, or casual event; a few accessories will elevate your look. This versatility is one of the reasons you should have a collection of essential jewelry. Here are some must-have basic jewelry items for every woman:

1. **Diamond earrings** are super classy and elegant. They are a great signature gem to add to your collection, budget permitting. Diamond earrings look good when you are out for brunch or heading for a big meeting. They shine radiantly and make

you look lovely for special family events or dates. This accessory is both classy and elegant.

2. **Pearl earrings and necklaces** are another jewelry staple. As beautiful and elegant as diamond earrings, it's always nice to have variety in your accessories. So, getting yourself a pair of simple pearls, an iconic alternative to diamond earrings, should be on your list! In addition, pearls will make you look more relaxed and low-key if that's the style you aim to achieve. Pearls have a way of making you look casual and switch your look when you want. Having pearl earrings and a necklace is as crucial as having a little black dress–the two complement each other perfectly. A pearl necklace is perfect for a graduation, anniversary dinner, or job interview.

3. **Simple sterling silver and 10K or 14K gold jewelry** are additional items you want to obtain for your collection. I suggest balls and hoops in varying sizes so they can be visible with different hairstyles. These specific metals are recommended for longevity and appearance. They can get wet without turning colors and can typically be worn even by those with sensitive

skin. These purchases also will be more pricey than their counterparts, but with proper care, they can last a lifetime and be passed down to others.

Other types of jewelry in those same metals to add to your collection are:

1. **Pendant necklaces**: A simple necklace with a thin chain that hangs a lovely pendant to your jewelry collection. The pendant is usually the big attraction, and the delicate chain complements the rest of your outfit. Pendant necklaces are beautiful and bold yet reserved.
2. **Chokers**: Necklaces that hug the neck and throat areas are called chokers. They are available in silver, gold, and bronze. Chokers can dress up a simple look, add flair to a casual outfit, or take a dressy outfit to another level.
3. **Bracelets**: Jewelry for your arms and wrists can significantly enhance your look. Bracelets come in different designs, sizes, and shapes. Some women can have one or two bracelets they never take off; others choose to wear them only on

special occasions. Again, I suggest getting these in metals for longevity.

4. **Rings**: A time-honored tradition exists of women adorning their fingers with all types of jewelry. In addition to metals, another staple for you to consider is rings with gemstones. Birthstones, diamonds, and trendy gems can make incredible collector items and pair well with your wardrobe for decades.

5. **Watches:** it doesn't matter what occasion it is or whether you are stepping out in a cozy or party outfit; watches never go out of style. There is something about a watch that completes your look and can make you look organized, confident, and sophisticated. Take your time and get one in your budget. Additionally, don't forget about accessorizing your digital companion. Many women choose Apple Watch, Fitbits, and others to help track health, stay organized, communicate without needing their phone/tablet/computer, and do mindfulness activities. If you decide that a digital timepiece is for you, consider getting watch bands in different colors and styles to

accessorize your outfits and take your watch from dressy to casual and vice versa.

Overall, the best style is *your style*! No look is complete without an accessory or a few complimentary pieces. The beauty of accessories is choosing one that fits your personality and style best. With these suggestions at hand, you will feel comfortable and confident in your look. Keep reading to learn how to build a wardrobe that makes you feel good while you are out and about rocking those pieces!

CHAPTER 6:

Unforgettable You–
Creating Your Signature Look

Mastering Your Looks

There are multiple aspects to creating a signature look. We have already discussed signature items and classics that you should add to your wardrobe (chapter 3). Now, we are going to elaborate more on your signature look.

Mastering your appearance so that you always look good may seem impossible at first. However, I assure you that once you decide what your "everyday look" will be, your "professional/career" and "dressy" signature looks will be so much easier to put together.

I share some big-picture thoughts below, but there are some other styles for your consideration. One of those is eclectic and/or artistic looks. I have a daughter who lives in D.C. Over time, I have seen her put together some combinations I would have never imagined. Still, she rarely misses "giving it to people!" I consider myself a fashionista, but I don't know where to begin assembling her looks.

Often, artists are like that, especially ones living in large cities. There are a lot of influences that smaller cities and more rural areas are not exposed to, like many urban dwellers. So, geographical location is often a factor not only for style but also for types of clothing.

Some of the warmest, most fashionable boots I acquired came from being out in Indiana in the dead of winter. The shoes sold in the discount retailers differ from the same stores in Georgia and North Carolina, where I travel the most. The same is true for warm-weather places. I have another daughter who is attending school in Florida. While visiting, I bought some of the cutest sandals I have ever seen because sandals are a specialty in warmer climates.

Purchases like these further prove my point: our location, climate, age, and access to different cultures will also contribute to our design style. My life was forever changed once I decided I was going to mostly wear tracksuits unless I was doing something for business or work. Although having daughters will alter your style, too—my daughter said one of my tracksuits made me look like a mafia boss, and I haven't worn some of them since! I got a good laugh at that comment, but nonetheless, I pressed on with my fashion choices–the same can be true for you.

Another contributing factor to my wardrobe was my two athletic daughters. While supporting them, I always found myself on a track, in the stands, or at a sports event. After a while, I gave up my boots (the only kind of shoes I used to wear when it finally got cold in the south) and bought sneakers that matched the girls' teams. I had changes based on my everyday needs and lifestyle routine. Likewise, I encourage you to do what works for you! As you read, keep the following factors in mind.

Everyday Wardrobe (Athleisure)

Let's discuss the perfect blend of comfort and style: the athleisure trend. Here's how you add fashion effortlessly to your everyday comfortable clothes. Hectic lifestyles require more comfortable and convenient clothing than ever before. As a working woman with many clients to cater to, you need to look great and feel relaxed. So how do you blend the two and not be at your wit's end? Let me explain.

The solution is athletic wear. Athleisure blurs the distinction between gym clothes and what you would wear to lunch simply by converting athletic clothing into everyday wear. Your clothing may accommodate going to the dancing studio and hitting the streets for a power show. Athleisure is trending; the reason? You can carry one look to your gym and an after-work drinking session without missing a beat. Why take an extra pair of work clothing when athleisure has your back?

You can effortlessly create a well-balanced outfit by matching your trendy wear and accessories, such as shoes, sweatpants, or a sports bra, with activewear items like trousers, a leather jacket, or heels. Athleisure is a brilliant investment to upgrade your work and everyday wardrobe. In particular, a high-performance fabric combined with a fashionable look is a great option.

Athleisure may be a brilliant choice for daily wear, but make sure you know the difference between it and business attire. You can successfully wear athleisure out of the gym to casual events like an outing with friends, after-work gatherings, etc., but wearing it to an official meeting or a family gathering like a wedding would be committing fashion suicide.

To pull off your athleisure looks in multiple settings, you need accessories. There is a method to pull this off and impress people with your fashion game. First, maintain a sleek, sporty atmosphere while incorporating a little bling. Second, wear jewelry, but don't go overboard; add sturdy studs, a watch, and a delicate bracelet to pull off the look. Third, a trendy bag, baseball cap, or aviator sunglasses will do. Next, to add a street-style touch to your athleisure, wear a slender chain and hoop earrings to your attire. Experimenting with different accessories and a little "swag" will take a long time. Be confident in what you do; soon, you will become the game master!

Signature Wardrobe (Capsule)

In today's fast fashion world, it's easy to accumulate too many outfits. These may not necessarily express our style or portray who we are. In the end, these add to the already massive landfills.

It's time to become mindful of what we "eye and buy". A carefully put-together capsule wardrobe creates a style ecology that you can mix and match endlessly. A capsule outfit typically comprises straight-leg denim, a khaki trench coat, and a staple sweater. You can play around with textures and colors within those basic guidelines to achieve the look that portrays the real you.

Moreover, wearing fewer, higher-quality clothes is a step towards a more sustainable wardrobe. It's unnecessary to constantly look for novelty when you can creatively remix your favorite pieces and look flawlessly fashionable. Understanding your body's proportions and the suitable prints and patterns will also help you look stylish. Creating a capsule wardrobe requires determination, proper analysis, and patience. Knowing what works for you is key to creating a great capsule wardrobe.

Capsule wardrobes are making waves in the fashion world. A compact wardrobe built from basic and classic styles, adding trendy accessories to give your outfit a simple but dapper touch, is how you ace fashion. The capsule wardrobe seemed to be the answer to everyone's fashion woes, especially during the recession—a furious decade of fast fashion that was wearing out our closets. Since then, social media has increasingly become a contributing factor.

Career Wardrobe (Classic Pieces/Colors)

As standards for professional dresses change rapidly, it's becoming more complex to determine what looks good and what doesn't. The goal of a skilled work wardrobe is to enable you to save time getting ready in the morning. In addition, it makes it more painless to put together multiple outfits with a few simple yet versatile changes. Achieving chic isn't hard if you step out of your comfort zone and are ready to try something different.

The standard career wardrobe has twenty essential pieces, including three outerwear items, three bottoms, four tops, one dress, three pairs of shoes, and six accessories. This count will help you put together a variety of chic work looks. It can contain classic styles that are simple to pair together for looks appropriate for the office and after work. Many of these items may already exist in your wardrobe.

If you live in a cold area, expand your outfit with warm apparel: add a woolen cap or a trench coat to your winter wardrobe. Wear a pair of tights underneath skirts or dresses for extra warmth. Replace the heels with knee-high or ankle-high boots. Likewise, replace long sleeves and sweaters with tank tops and short sleeves as soon as summer arrives.

For a warmer environment, choose breathable outerwear, such as light jackets and linen blazers. In the summer, having an additional dress or skirt can be helpful. Add a few more T-shirts and tank tops to function as layering items. Layering is yet another way of adding points of interest to your attire.

Additionally, before you start shopping, you must consider your workplace's dress code. If your workplace has a relaxed dress code, add one or two pairs of jeans to your work wardrobe. If your profession requires more movement, switch out the heels for flats. Hustling in heels is a big NO if you want to look comfortable and do your best at work.

Making a classic professional career wardrobe doesn't require you to stock your closet with boring essentials. Include items that express your unique character. Upgrade your neutral-hued look with vibrant coats/blazers and boldly patterned blouses.

Replace oversized coats with fitted cardigans, midi skirts with straight-leg slacks, and gold jewelry with a trendy silver one. Create a unique look for yourself by personalizing your clothing.

Start by investing in neutral colors like black, white, gray, camel, beige, etc., as these will enable you to create more classic outfits with fewer pieces. Once you have mastered the classic look, pick one or two accent hues to add a statement to your appearance. Dark hues like burnt orange, emerald green, and mustard yellow are perfect for a fall or winter work outfit. Try lighter shades like powder blue, blush pink, or lilac for your work outfit in the spring or summer.

If you like an all-neutral color palette, choose color-neutral items in exciting patterns like leopard print, houndstooth, stripes, plaid, or floral to broaden your looks. These staples are always helpful to have at hand, whether you're starting a business, looking for a new job, or simply updating your professional dress wardrobe. For all occasions, keep these things ready to create the best professional look in minutes.

Bonus Section

At the beginning of the book, I told you that we had two chapters heavily influenced by a master makeup artist and an incredible certified hair care professional. You may wonder why I included them in a book about creating a killer wardrobe within your budget. I learned during my journey that after I got my clothes together, there were three more components to achieving unshakeable confidence. Those elements were my skin, makeup, and hair.

I wish someone had told me that if I took better care of my skin, I wouldn't need as much makeup, but I didn't learn this lesson until later in life. We live in a time when we know about hydration and nutrition's role in healthy skin. However, if you are plagued with breakouts, dark circles, and other issues, guess what? We created this section for you!

As you continue to read, you will gain further insight into skincare and much more.

Creating a schedule for my hair was the final game changer to elevating my look. Your schedule will look different depending on your hair type, texture, and style, but protective styles have become life savers for me. Although my hectic schedule, night sweats, and tender-headedness made me a lousy candidate for going natural, I still desired to reduce the number of relaxers that I got per year. I reduced that number from nine to five by adopting a schedule that fluctuated between wearing my hair old, weaves, wigs, and braids. For me, braids in the summer and wigs/weaves in the winter were a winner.

Hair solutions will vary for everyone, but the key is to find a system that works for you so you can show up confidently (literally) from head to toe! So, let's jump into these final pages.

CHAPTER 7

The Foundation of Beautiful Makeup Starts with Intentional Skincare

Somanetha Moulate (Sommie) explains in this chapter why the foundation of beautiful makeup is intentional skincare!

Skin Care: The Canvas for Your Makeup

In my experience, the foundation of flawless makeup begins with healthy, well-cared-for skin. Think of your face as a canvas: if the canvas is not smooth and prepared, the final artwork will never achieve its full potential. Whether working with brides or doing makeup consultations for upcoming events, one of my first pieces of advice is always the same:

invest in your skincare routine. Healthy skin provides the best base for makeup, essential for achieving that glowing, radiant look we all want.

A consistent skincare regimen is vital. While everyone's skin is different, a few basic steps should form the backbone of your daily routine. These steps include:

6. **Cleansing**: removes dirt, oil, and impurities that accumulate on the skin throughout the day. Clean skin allows your skincare products and makeup to perform better and last longer.
7. **Toning**: helps balance the skin's pH and tightens pores, ensuring your skin is prepped for moisturizing and further treatment. It's an important step that many overlook, but it truly helps set the stage for the next steps.
8. **Moisturizing**: hydration is key. No matter your skin type, moisturizer helps maintain the skin's moisture barrier, preventing it from becoming dry or irritated. Well-hydrated skin provides the smoothest base for foundation and other makeup products.

These three steps may seem simple, but they make a difference in your skin's health and your makeup's longevity. The better your skin feels, the better your makeup will look and stay in place throughout the day.

One common concern I often hear from clients is that they avoid moisturizing because they fear it will make their skin look oily or shiny. I completely understand this worry, but I always advise that excess oil is a sign that your skin is trying to protect itself from dehydration. If your skin isn't getting enough moisture, it will compensate by overproducing oil. By following a balanced skincare routine with moisturizing as a key step, you can reduce the appearance of excess oil over time.

Additionally, I recognize that many people have skin concerns beyond hydration. Some issues include:

- Broken blood vessels (spider veins)
- Hyperpigmentation
- Melasma
- Dark circles
- Rosacea

- Acne
- Dry or oily skin
- Eye bags

These concerns can stem from a variety of causes, including genetics, hormones, or environmental factors. If you're dealing with any of these issues, it's best to seek advice from a dermatologist who can recommend treatments or solutions tailored to your needs.

Makeup: Enhancing What You Already Have

While skincare provides the foundation for beautiful skin, makeup is the perfect tool to enhance and address specific concerns, creating a polished and confident look. Makeup is transformative—it can conceal, highlight, and define, allowing you to create whatever look you desire.

Take me for example. From a young age, I've always had a natural talent for sketching and drawing. I've carried this skill into my makeup artistry, but I also recognize that technology has revolutionized the makeup world. Today, you don't need to be an artist to master makeup. With the right products and techniques, anyone can create a stunning look.

The makeup world is incredibly diverse, with endless possibilities to experiment and express yourself. Every woman has preferences regarding how much or how little makeup she wants to apply. For many women, the goal is to cover up blemishes or skin concerns in the morning. Others prefer a more enhanced or glamorous look. No matter the intention, achieving a polished look in 5–10 minutes is possible with the right products. Here's a simple morning routine for a natural yet put-together look:

1. **Moisturizer** (to hydrate the skin and provide a smooth base)
2. **Primer** (to ensure long-lasting makeup)
3. **Eyes and Brows** (enhancing the eyes and shaping the brows)
4. **Foundation or CC Cream** (for an even complexion)
5. **Concealer** (to cover any blemishes or dark circles)
6. **Setting Powder** (to set everything in place and prevent shine)

7. **Bronzer** (to add warmth and definition)
8. **Blush** (to give a natural flush of color)
9. **Mascara and Liner** (to define the eyes)
10. **Lipstick or Lip Gloss** (to complete the look)

With just a few products and a little blending, you can be out the door in no time, feeling confident and fresh.

However, when clients ask me why their makeup looks different when they do it themselves compared to a professional makeup artist, I always explain the difference: technique, products, and lighting. When I work with clients for weddings, photo shoots, or special events, we use a more extensive range of products and techniques to achieve that flawless, camera-ready look. Professional makeup artists often use more concentrated formulas designed to withstand high-definition cameras and long hours under hot studio lights. The blending, shading, and layering that go into creating a professional look take time and precision. Eyeshadow, for example, may involve multiple pigments, glitter, or intricate shading, all of which require careful application.

One key factor in professional makeup is lighting. Lighting plays a massive role in how makeup appears on camera or in person. The proper lighting can make a dramatic difference in how your makeup looks and holds up throughout the day. Lighting effects are why makeup applied at home may look slightly different than what you'd see in professional photoshoots or events, where high-end products and strategic lighting create a polished, long-lasting effect.

The Fun of Makeup: Embrace Your Style

Makeup is not just a tool—it's an art form and a way to express yourself. Whether you're a busy corporate mom on the go, an entrepreneur building her brand, or anyone in between, finding makeup routines and looks that suit your lifestyle is just as important as finding the right outfits.

Remember, you don't have to figure out your skincare or makeup journey on your own. If you're unsure where to start or how to improve, you don't have to navigate it alone. That's where professionals like myself come in! Whether you need advice, tips, or a complete makeover, we're here to support you on your journey to beautiful, confident skin and makeup.

Book with Sommie: ***http://hxprofessional.com***
Follow Sommie on IG: @simplysommie

CHAPTER 8:

Mastering Your Mane: Hair Care for Busy Women

As I shared in the bonus introduction, the final game changer to elevating my look was creating a schedule for my hair. Let me start by saying this: please try to find a hairstylist who fits your needs and understands your lifestyle, especially if you do not know how to do hair or want to learn. Develop a relationship with your stylist and work together to develop a consistent routine. This may take some time and trial and error, but it's ultimately worth it! Over time, I created a hair team to help me manage my needs. In the meantime, while on your search for a stylist, here are a few tips from one of my "hair heroes"—Ashley Brooks!

1. **Shampoo your hair every one to two weeks and try to do it on the same day to build consistency.** Sweat, dust, dead skin, and excess products dirty our hair. And if it's not cleaned frequently, the scalp can become itchy and flaky. Therefore, the first step of your routine should be washing your hair. As a busy woman, you can do this once every two weeks. Please give it a deep wash with a quality shampoo and conditioner, then moisturize it.

   This process will help your hair to be clean, healthy, and grow. When you wash your natural hair too frequently, you remove its natural oils, leaving it dry, dull, and rough. Thus, once in two weeks is perfect. But if you feel your hair is too dirty from a lot of product build-up, you can wash it once a week.

2. **Use a hair mask or moisturizing treatment. Apply from ends to roots, avoiding the scalp.** This treatment hydrates hair and makes it shinier and more potent, thus reducing breakage. A hair mask should be a significant part of a busy woman's routine because it gives hair extra

nutrients and moisture that lasts a while. A hair mask should be applied after shampooing and rinsing. Shampoo usually opens hair follicles. When you use a mask, your hair absorbs it entirely. Apply the mask to your damp hair from the roots to the tips. Leave it on (between three to twenty minutes, depending on how damaged your hair is), then rinse it off. The duration will also be indicated on the mask you're using.

Afterward, your hair will feel smooth, silky, and healthy. You can do this when giving your hair a complete wash, once in two weeks or once a week if that's how frequently you wash your hair. Different types of masks, from creamy to light, depend on your hair type and what you're trying to achieve.

3. **Style your hair at night to prepare for the following day.** For example, if you wear your hair straight or curled and your shampoo day is Monday, you should shampoo, blow dry, and style your hair Monday evening. Upon styling, pin curl, roll, flexi rod, or wrap to preserve your hair every night.

For my natural girls, I advise that you do your braid-outs and twists at night. Also, an extra tip: if you blow dry or stretch your hair before twisting, your set will have less frizz and better control when twisting.

If you're like me, your morning is packed, and you don't have enough time to straighten your hair. If that's the case, you can do this at night before sleep. Take time to detangle your hair and straighten it as you watch a movie before bed or while sipping tea or wine. After this, tie your hair loosely using a scrunchy or pin it up and wrap it in a satin bonnet while you sleep. It will then take you less time to get ready in the morning.

4. **Embrace protective styling.** If you leave your hair open for a long time, it can break and have split ends. This is where protective styling comes in. Protective styles keep your hair concealed and require little to no manipulation. Since you won't do much to your hair when you have these styles, your hair doesn't break because of less stretching and pulling.

Your hair becomes healthy since the moisture is locked in as opposed to when your hair is exposed to cold and heat. Additionally, it leaves you with more time to spend on other activities. Protective styles are a great hair routine for busy women. There are several types of protective styles you can try. Examples include braids, twists, cornrows, and wigs. Please read below for more details:

a. ***Knotless braids***: these have gained popularity because they are stylish and versatile. Moreover, they don't add stress and tension to your scalp because they don't involve making knots at the root of your hair. You can create an elegant updo with it, let it flow down your back, or hold some braids together and allow a few to hang.

b. ***Cornrows***: this is one of the most straightforward protective hairstyles you can have. They are stylish, easy to braid, and low maintenance. Your hairdressers can also do variations of the normal cornrows. For example, you can try cornrows with a faux pony or a low bun.

c. **Twists**: there are so many types of twists you can experiment with. Examples include flat twists, jumbo twists, Marley twists, passion twists, or pony and flat twists. They are simple and take less time to create, which is perfect for you if you have a lot on your plate.

d. **Faux locs**: getting traditional locs done takes a long time and requires lots of maintenance. So, if you like the locs look but don't want to make the commitment that comes with it, you can try faux locs. Also, they keep your hair tucked away and, therefore, safe from breakage from combing, heat, etc. You don't need to wash your hair when you have them; they're also low maintenance.

e. **Crochet braids**: cover your scalp and protect your edges. They're also easy to moisturize your hair while you have them. You can create them differently depending on what you want to crochet on your cornrows.

f. **Wigs** can be a great protective style if your cornrows are not braided tightly. However, when the cornrows are incredibly tight, they pull at your hair, which we are trying to avoid.

Also, frequently using glue when installing some lace-front wigs can cause tension on your edges, which can start thinning. So consider these factors if you want wigs as a protective style.

g. **Weaves**: Sew-in weaves are an excellent hair routine for busy women because they take less time to install. The cornrows (braided underneath the weave) protect your natural hair from damage from environmental factors like heat and pollutants. Additionally, they will help you get ready faster than if you had to style your natural hair whenever you leave the house. However, it is essential to note that weaves are only protective hairstyles if excessive pulling isn't involved when installing them.

Furthermore, having protective styles is not an excuse to neglect your hair. Instead, they give your hair a break from the pulling and help you look presentable when you have a busy schedule. You still need to remove the style (after a while) and take care of your hair underneath. You can clean your hair with protective styles after 2 to 3 weeks. When washing them, you should concentrate more on your scalp.

Strong & Healthy Hair is Within Your Reach

A hair routine for busy women is a lifesaver because it helps us take good care of our hair, maintain our appearance, and manage other life responsibilities. As you've seen from this chapter, haircare doesn't have to be complicated. You can pick two weekends in a month to wash your hair and apply a mask. When you throw in dry shampoo and straighten your hair at night, you'll have an easier time in the morning. You can then use a leave-in conditioner to give your hair a fresh look.

Once in a while, it's okay to give yourself (and your hair) a break by having protective styles. Use this simple hair routine to ensure you look good and keep your hair strong and healthy. And again, if it fits your budget and you don't have the time or patience to manage your mane, find a stylist to help you grow and nurture your hair. We exist to help women love their hair.

Book with Ashley: **http://ashleysquared.com**
Follow Ashley on IG: @_ashleysquared

Conclusion

This book was written to give you the tools to slay your look today and for years to come! Trends come and go, but your signature style will help you look good no matter what. I cannot overstate the importance of loving how you look. It is often the catalyst needed to effect the positive change you have been seeking.

While I know that looks are not everything, they are vitally important because they typically directly relate to your confidence, which can make or break so many aspects of life. Please know that I am cheering for you! My journey, which started so tough, changed drastically. I went from being a single mom with four children to happily remarried with two bonus children and six grandchildren (and counting)!

If you are a mom who is struggling with post-partum depression, I want to encourage you that there is joy on the other side of the pain. If you are fighting to break free from a toxic relationship, there is more for you than the person who is psychologically or physically abusing you. If you are just a busy mom and wife and have no time for yourself, I beg you to *make time*! There is only one you; if you go down, the *whole ship goes down, baby*! And if you are single and haven't felt like yourself, I dare you to attack that closet, create a budget, and start building a wardrobe you love! It can be the missing puzzle piece for everything else to fall into place.

I am passionate about women looking and feeling their best. If you want to learn more about our services, please visit ***http://rainahdavis.com***. Until next time, I pray love, peace, and blessings over each of you!

—*Rainah*

www.ingramcontent.com/pod-product-compliance
Lightning Source LLC
Chambersburg PA
CBHW060937120626
46557CB00003B/1036